I'm Happy when It's Cloudy

Our Journey Through BiPolar Disorder

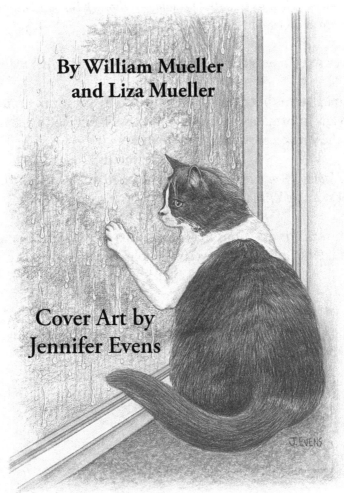

By William Mueller
and Liza Mueller

Cover Art by
Jennifer Evens

 Pine Creek & Northwestern PublishingCompany

Statistics printed within these pages are provided with permission from The National Alliance on Mental Illness, NAMI

Pine Creek & Northwestern Publishing Company
is located in Minnesota

ISBN13: 978-1-937162-18-4

Library of Congress Control Number: 2021949505

Mental Illness

If you have questions about a statistic or term that's being used, please visit the original study.

1 in 5 U.S. adults experience mental illness each year

1 in 20 U.S. adults experience serious mental illness each year

1 in 6 U.S. youth aged 6-17 experience a mental health disorder each year

50% of all lifetime mental illness begins by age 14, and 75% by age 24

Suicide is the 2nd leading cause of death among people aged 10-34

20.6% of U.S. adults experienced mental illness in 2019 (51.5 million people). This represents 1 in 5 adults.

5.2% of U.S. adults experienced serious mental illness in 2019 (13.1 million people). This represents 1 in 20 adults.

16.5% of U.S. youth aged 6-17 experienced a mental health disorder in 2016 (7.7 million people)

3.8% of U.S. adults experienced a co-occurring substance use disorder and mental illness in 2019 (9.5 million people)

Annual prevalence of mental illness among U.S. adults, by demographic group:

Non-Hispanic Asian: 14.4%. Non-Hispanic white: 22.2%

Non-Hispanic black or African-American: 17.3%

Non-Hispanic American Indian or Alaska Native: 18.7%

Non-Hispanic mixed/multiracial: 31.7%

Non-Hispanic Native Hawaiian or Other Pacific Islander: 16.6%

Hispanic or Latino: 18.0%

Lesbian, Gay or Bisexual: 44.1%

Annual prevalence among U.S. adults, by condition:

Major Depressive Episode: 7.8% (19.4 million people)

Schizophrenia: <1% (estimated 1.5 million people)

Bipolar Disorder: 2.8% (estimated 7 million people)

Anxiety Disorders: 19.1% (estimated 48 million people)

Posttraumatic Stress Disorder: 3.6% (estimated 9 million people)

Obsessive Compulsive Disorder: 1.2% (estimated 3 million people)

Borderline Personality Disorder: 1.4% (estimated 3.5 million people)

Mental Health Care Matters in 2019

44.8% of U.S. adults with mental illness received treatment

65.5% of U.S. adults with serious mental illness received treatment

50.6% of U.S. youth aged 6-17 with a mental health disorder received treatment in 2016

The average delay between onset of mental illness symptoms and treatment is 11 years

Annual treatment rates among U.S. adults with any mental illness, by demographic group in 2019:

Male: 36.8%, Female: 49.7%, Lesbian, Gay or Bisexual: 49.2%

Non-Hispanic Asian: 23.3%, Non-Hispanic white: 50.3%

Non-Hispanic black or African-American: 32.9%

Non-Hispanic mixed/multiracial: 43.0%, Hispanic or Latino: 33.9%

10.9% of U.S. adults with mental illness had no insurance coverage.

11.9% of U.S. adults with serious mental illness had no insurance.

55% of U.S. counties do not have a single practicing psychiatrist

The Ripple Effect Of Mental Illness

PERSON

People with depression have a 40% higher risk of developing cardiovascular and metabolic diseases than the general population. People with serious mental illness are nearly twice as likely to develop these conditions.

18.4% of U.S. adults with mental illness also experienced a substance use disorder in 2019 (9.5 million individuals)

The rate of unemployment is higher among U.S. adults who have mental illness (5.8%) compared to those who do not (3.6%)

High school students with significant symptoms of depression are more than twice as likely to drop out compared to their peers

Students aged 6-17 with mental, emotional or behavioral concerns are 3 times more likely to repeat a grade.

FAMILY

At least 8.4 million people in the U.S. provide care to an adult with a mental or emotional health issue

Caregivers of adults with mental or emotional health issues spend an average of 32 hours per week providing unpaid care

COMMUNITY

Mental illness and substance use disorders are involved in 1 out of every 8 emergency department visits by a U.S. adult (estimated 12 million visits)

Mood disorders are the most common cause of hospitalization for all people in the U.S. under age 45 (after excluding hospitalization relating to pregnancy and birth)

Across the U.S. economy, serious mental illness causes $193.2 billion in lost earnings each year

20.5% of people experiencing homelessness in the U.S. have a serious mental health condition

37% of adults incarcerated in the state and federal prison system have a diagnosed mental illness

70.4% of youth in the juvenile justice system have a diagnosed mental illness

41% of Veteran's Health Administration patients have a diagnosed mental illness or substance use disorder

WORLD

Depression and anxiety disorders cost the global economy $1 trillion in lost productivity each year

Depression is a leading cause of disability worldwide

It's Okay To Talk About Suicide

Suicide is the 2nd leading cause of death for ages 10-34 in the U.S.

Suicide is the 10th leading cause of death in the U.S.

The overall suicide rate in the U.S. has increased by 35% since 1999

46% who die by suicide had a diagnosed mental health condition

90% of people who die by suicide had shown symptoms of a mental health condition, according to interviews with family, friends and medical professionals (also known as psychological autopsy)

Lesbian, gay and bisexual youth are 4 times more likely to attempt suicide than straight youth

78% of people who die by suicide are male

Trans gender adults are nearly 12 times more likely to attempt suicide than the general population

Annual prevalence of serious thoughts of suicide, by U.S. demographic group:

All adults 4.8%,

Aged 18-25 11.8%,

High school students 18.8%,

Lesbian, gay, and bisexual high school students 46.8%

If you or someone you know is in an emergency, call

The National Suicide Prevention Lifeline at 800-273-TALK (8255) or call 911 immediately.

MENTAL ILLNESS AND THE CRIMINAL JUSTICE SYSTEM

About 2 million times each year, people with serious mental illness are booked into jails.

About 2 in 5 people who are incarcerated have a history of mental illness (37% in state and federal prisons and 44% held in local jails).

66% of women in prison reported having a history of mental illness, almost twice the percentage of men in prison.

Nearly one in four people shot and killed by police officers between 2015 and 2020 had a mental health condition.

Suicide is the leading cause of death for people held in local jails.

An estimated 4,000 people with serious mental illness are held in solitary confinement inside U.S. prisons.

COMMUNITIES

70% of youth in the juvenile justice system have a diagnosable mental health condition.

Youth in detention are 10 times more likely to suffer from psychosis than youth in the community.

About 50,000 veterans are held in local jails — 55% report experiencing a mental illness.

Among incarcerated people with a mental health condition, non-white individuals are more likely to go to solitary confinement, be injured, and stay longer in jail.

ACCESS TO CARE

About 3 in 5 people (63%) with a history of mental illness do not receive mental health treatment while incarcerated in state and federal prisons.

Less than half of people (45%) with a history of mental illness receive mental health treatment while held in local jails.

People who have healthcare coverage upon release from incarceration are more likely to engage in services that reduce recidivism.

Last updated: Mar. 2021

Call the NAMI Helpline at 800-950-NAMI if in a crisis

These Statistics printed with permission of The National Alliance on Mental Illness, NAMI

Acknowledgements

William and I would like to thank the following people:

Jennifer Evens for your amazing cover art.

Steve Delisi for your knowledge, help, and time.

Tylar and Raissa Mueller for your unconditional love and understanding.

A special thank you to Katie Gue for her creative contribution to our logo.

Our parents, Tom & Lois Gunther and Dale & Marilyn Mueller for your love, support, guidance, and time.

And Edna Siniff. A heartfelt thank you for sharing your amazing knowledge and creative gifts with us. Your patience, your time and guidance. And most of all for believing in this book. *I Am Happy When It's Cloudy* may not have been written without out your support.

Thank you all for joining us on our journey.

Peace and Love ,

William and Liza Mueller

William and Natalie

I'm Happy When It's Cloudy

William Mueller 2021

I'm Happy When It's Cloudy has been written over the course of many years of experience with bipolar disorder and mental illness. This book is not to entertain or disturb its readers. Its to educate the reader on some of the thought processes that are present in the illness.

Seattle sees a lot of rain, and there are some that are happy about that and some not. I am happy when it rains or is cloudy. The happy events occur in life, but those days are the cloudy days of my life. Clear days can be a disappointment for me.

I was first diagnosed with Bipolar disorder in 2000 and put on depakote and seroquel. I was on medications during 2009 until I could not afford my medications and came off them for a brief period. I could not secure county assistance. I would not recommend going without medication.

In August of 2009 I was hospitalized for 15 days and a complete reevaluation was undertaken. A new medication was added, ziprasidone. And a new diagnosis came forth, bipolar type 2 and schizoaffective disorder. I was sent to a group home for 3 months and an assisted living facility for two years. I thought my life was basically over.

A social worker told me when I moved into the facility, that I would never live on my own or work again. When I first heard that, I really thought things were over. But after much thought on what I had been through in life, I said to myself, this would not occur. And that I would pray and work hard to get out on my own and work again.

It took two years, but I eventually found a full time job and moved into a townhome in Coon Rapids, MN. That was 2011. I lived there for about 3 years. I met my wife online and moved to Eagan, MN in 2014.

I obtained my commercial drivers license July 2016, got married in October 2016. and still reside in Eagan as of today.

I drive a truck for a living now. I also have been certified by the

Minnesota transportation museum as a student brakeman for a tourist railroad operation.

So, there is hope for people with a mental illness.

I recommend getting a medical doctor-psychiatrist as they know best what to look for and prescribe. From 2008 until present day I have been writing about the experience through my journey with these mental illnesses and the challenges of the mind and life that is lived.

Some parts of these writings are dark, some seem hopeless and some painful. And it is in most cases. My only saving grace is my family, friends and faith that have seen me through this time. And their constant love and support to live day by day, sometimes minute by minute.

Personal Solutions Beyond Medicine

Personal solutions usually get overlooked when addressing mental illness. While medications and therapy are good starts, there are other practical ways to cope.

Oncoming episodes may not be apparent to the individual who is contending with mental illness. The people closest to them may see the oncoming depression, or manic side before it is felt by the diagnosed person.

Music helps soothe my mind. Listening to a song that has a purpose and meaning brings me out of depression. Oftentimes I find inspiration in the music I listen to. This draws out the pain and other emotions I'm feeling.

Sometimes a hug from my wife or encouraging words of praise from her lifts my spirits. My relationship with Natalie our pet cat helps distract me from my bipolar world and personal thoughts. Other things I enjoy are outdoor activities such as spending time with family, hiking, and fishing. It is important to me to take time out from my hectic world to go camping or visit a state park.

Another area of importance to me is establishing relationships, whether it be clubs, a church, or other organizations.

There is a whole world out there for us to explore, and so many people to get to know. We are never alone on this journey. And if you feel alone, reach out to someone, a friend, a family member, an organization or medical professionals to help you feel better and understand your journey.

We hope you become more aware of the journey of those who struggle with the controversial issues of mental illness. And we hope that you are inspired to reach out and advocate for those in need.

Thank you for reading and purchasing *I'm Happy When Its Cloudy*.

Liza and William

We are Living with Bipolar Disorder

Liza Mueller 2021

My husband is living with Bipolar Disorder. There, I said it out loud.

Somehow, I thought it would make our lives easier by saying bipolar, but it doesn't. As I am writing this, I am thinking to myself, "What have I learned about Bipolar Disorder?" Not nearly as much as I need to know. What I am learning is how not to beat myself up for not knowing what I think I need to know.

I have to be honest in saying that I was like a lot of people and had a very vague knowledge and understanding of what mental illness is. I was guided by the incorrect attitudes and stereotypes that mental illness is one size fits all. I had no idea that it was even a disease because people with mental illness were just crazy people. I felt sorry for them but didn't really understand what life might be like for a person living with mental illness. It was easier if I just didn't talk about it. Mental illness is an uncomfortable subject and historically people with any kind of mental illness were treated as having lesser intelligence, troubled souls who did not fit into the conventional stereotypes of what a normal person in society is. Today there are many different and specific combinations of mental illnesses. Previously all mental illness was just lumped together. Knowing what I know now I am embarrassed by my previous lack of knowledge and fear of talking about the mental illness taboo. I look back at the people who have come in and out of my life and think to myself "if I had taken the time to learn about and try to understand what having a mental illness was like, could I have helped just one person who lived secretly with a mental illness?"

That thought is a hard pill to swallow as I have always thought of myself as a non-judgmental person - a "to each his own" and "live and let live" attitude while totally avoiding things that made me uncomfortable. It has not been easy being out of my comfort zone but as I learn more about mental illness and continue on this journey with William, I feel blessed to have been given a second chance to make a difference in someone's life. And not making a difference so that I feel the glory of the action but making a difference because everyone deserves a chance to be heard, understood, and accepted and to live a healthy happy life.

In recent years the topic of mental illness has come to the forefront. Many celebrities living with different mental illnesses are stepping out to bring awareness. This is a good thing but there is so much more that needs to be said and learned regarding this topic. It seems a daunting task. My goal through this journey is to learn as much as I can about bipolar disorder so I can be a stabilizing person in William's life. I have learned that living with or being married to a person with Bipolar or any other mental illness is not the end of the world. Mental illness is a disease. We should be educated on it so we can help the people we love who are living with this disease to live a healthy and happy life.

It is time to break the archaic stereotype and educate ourselves. When a loved one is diagnosed with cancer what do we do? We educate ourselves about the type of cancer so we can be a support to our loved one during their cancer journey. And we educate others so that it brings awareness to the cause.

That right there has become my passion.

It is a lifelong journey with someone who is living with Bipolar Disorder or any mental illness. Both the person who is living with Bipolar and the spouse or family members living with that person all react differently to the highs and lows, and that is okay. I'm not going to lie— it isn't easy, and there are days that wear me out. There are days that break me down, days that scare me, and days that make me angry. However, there are days that I feel accomplished and I am proud of the things I have learned and conquered. Those days balance out this journey for me.

William was honest with me, up front, about his bipolar diagnosis early in our relationship. He gave me every opportunity to end things if his diagnosis was too much for me to handle. He told me about the medications he was taking and his experiences dealing with the disease. William was diligent taking his medications and keeping on top of things so I wasn't too worried because I thought if he was taking his medications that must keep the disease under control. This was all new to me when I met William. I knew that people had mental illness but quite honestly, I didn't realize how many people actually live with a mental illness.

What is Mental Illness and What causes it?

That's a fair question to ask but one that does not have one clear, concise answer.

Statistics

Webster's Dictionary defines Mental Illness as any disease of the mind; the psychological state of someone who has emotional or behavioral problems serious enough to require psychiatric intervention.

Okay, that is a pretty broad definition so let's be more specific.

Webster's Dictionary defines Bipolar Disorder as a noun, meaning a mental disorder characterized by episodes of mania and depression.

Symptoms: manic depression, manic depressive illness, manic depressive psychosis.

Well that is a little more specific but what causes this and more important how is it treated.

The Mayo Clinic website says that the exact cause of Bipolar Disorder is unknown. Mayo Clinic also states, "people with Bipolar Disorder appear to have physical changes in their brains." And "Bipolar Disorder is more common in people who have a first-degree relative such as a sibling or parent with the condition."

The Statistics on mental illness are eye opening.

According to **The National Alliance on Mental Illness** (NAMI) website

1 in 5 U.S. adults experience mental illness each year

1 in 25 U.S. adults experience serious mental illness each year

19.1% of U.S. adults experienced mental illness in 2018 (47.6 million people). This represents 1 in 5 adults.

4.6% of U.S. adults experienced serious mental illness in 2018 (11.4 million people). This represents 1 in 25 adults.

The **World Health Organization** reports Bipolar disorder is the sixth leading cause of disability in the world.

According to the Depression and Bipolar Support Alliance (DBSA, 2000) Consumers with bipolar disorder face up to ten years of coping with symptoms before getting accurate diagnosis, with only one in four receiving an accurate diagnosis in less than three years.

So, armed with this information I began my journey,

William and I dated three years and were married in the fall of 2016. Marriage had a big adjustment curve for me as I was older and getting married for the first time. I had many ideas of what a marriage should and would be like. Being an independent woman I just assumed that is how it would be. Marriage takes work.

First lesson learned:

I knew it would, I just didn't know that it would be as challenging for me as it was and is. Up until that point in my life I lived on my own, had my own home, a good job, and came and went as I pleased. I didn't have to answer to anyone and my life was all about me. It wasn't that I was a selfish person; it just took some time to incorporate marriage into my lifestyle. I was in control of everything in my house and in my life and that abruptly changed. I learned that I was a bit of a control freak—okay, a big control freak and I had to teach myself to let things go, pick my battles and that my way was not the only way and not necessarily the right way to accomplish any given task. Now, add a spouse with bipolar disorder to the mix, and that changes how you need to react to just about everything you face in life. As the spouse or partner of a person living with Bipolar Disorder it is easy to start to feel like a caregiver. I have felt that way at times, however, as I educate myself about the disease, and journey in married life with William I am learning to change that feeling. I am not his caregiver! I am his wife and together we support each other through this journey. It is not always easy, and as I mentioned before, I am new at this so I am always trying to grow and learn and understand more about the disease.

William is very good at living with his mental illness. When I say that I mean that society has taught him he has to mask the symptoms he faces during manic episodes. So, to most people he seems fine on the outside, when on the inside it seems as though his life is falling apart. That breaks my heart.

Some of the symptoms William deals with are crippling anxiety and paranoia. He has leaned to build walls to protect himself from a society that uses the words crazy and insane without giving a thought to who those words might hurt or offend. Think about that statement for a moment. Then for one day count the times you use those words to describe or react to something. I have— and it was a very interesting exercise. Now, if I am tempted to use those words carelessly, I take the time to find better words to use.

Second lesson learned:

One of the most important tools in any relationship is communication. It is even more important when you have a partner, spouse, or family member who is living with Bipolar Disorder. Learning about the disease, the symptoms, and the triggers affecting your loved one is paramount in keeping the lines of communication open and CLEAR. Each person with bipolar exhibits symptoms differently and reacts to them differently.

I have learned to read between the lines with William and understand what his is saying or isn't saying, so that I can keep one step ahead of this disease. I have learned to listen carefully and ask clarifying questions when things seem off. Triggers for cycling into different manic or depressive episodes are very individual. It is important to learn and watch for your loved one's triggers. Knowing them makes it possible to support and advocate during episodes. Triggers can be anything from stress from a job, a change in seasons (holidays can be a difficult time), or a traumatic event in one's life such as a divorce or death of someone close. If you can recognize these triggers you can ask the right clarifying questions when you see your spouse or loved one exhibiting a change in their normal behavior and that if caught early enough makes it easier to navigate through the cycling periods and ultimately plan ahead for the next bipolar hurdle. I continue to learn to read the subtle signs that something is not right with how he is feeling. And he is learning to trust me knowing that I am not going to judge him, but I am here to journey with him and be the support he needs.

We are learning together to take advantage of the quiet times and make plans for things when he begins to cycle through a bipolar episode.

For example, finances. One of the classic symptoms in a manic episode is impulsive spending. Finances in general can be stressful for married couples, especially having to combine finances when newly married. For the two of us it was no different. We came into our relationship with separate bank accounts and bills and "baggage" and had to work together to combine them in a way that would work best for us. We have our main bank account where both of our paychecks are automatically deposited, and all household bills and expenses are paid from. I have a separate account that is in my name only and I am able to move money into that account so that he does not have access to it. We agreed this would be important to have so that he still has access to our account and can use it, but during manic episodes I am able to move money so that bills are paid and which limits the amount he can spend. I have alerts set up on the main account that tell me when purchases of preset amount ate being made so that I can monitor the balance quickly and easily. We also have a monthly calendar and spreadsheet so that we have a visual reminder on what is coming in and what is going out. It is important to have these types of conversations ahead of time so that you can agree upon different options and processes and have things set up so that when you are dealing with the bipolar cycle you are not feeling out of control. Planning ahead is critical

Social Media is something we all use however, it can be an issue during certain times, and is one of the things I monitor to stay ahead of when William is cycling through his illness. If I see unusual posts or behaviors, I know that he could be going into a manic episode. I have learned that if I approach his social media posting in a non-accusing manner, listen, and ask the right clarifying questions, together we can determine if a medication check is needed. Sometimes it is just simply turning off the electronics and talking about what is causing his stress. That goes both ways — I find that I am connected to electronics more now since this Corona Virus quarantine. Watching for triggers in social media, television watching or changes in other daily functions keeps us one step ahead. If the episode is caught early William and I are usually able to discuss how he is feeling and what has changed for him. That allows me to be a strong support for him, and to be someone he feels safe with no matter what is happening. And he does the same for me.

Words, I love words. They can be straight forward as basic communication— Today is Friday. Or words can be beautiful— the sunlight kissed the gossamer wings of the dragonfly. Words can also be cutting when misused or taken out of context. There are different kinds of people who use words differently as well — straight forward thinkers, poets and playful people. One of the most important things I have learned through this journey is how to use my words more effectively so that I can still maintain my playful personality and communicate without being hurtful. Take a moment and think about a recent argument or heated discussion you had with someone in your life living with a mental illness. What words did you choose to use and what tone did you have? Every married couple is going to have these little things that happen that annoy each other.

I have learned to choose my words carefully. That is such a cliché, but so true. Why does this matter? It matters because depending on how William is dealing with the challenges of the outside world, my petty or sarcastic words may cause him to feel like he can't do anything right and why should he even try.

Words are important and need to be used wisely with anyone and especially with a spouse living with Bipolar Disorder. I can be having a bad day and snap at him about a trivial issue, some quirky behavior of his that annoys me, and it changes from me being in a bad mood and venting to my spouse, to him feeling like everything he does is wrong. Was venting my frustration in a negative way helpful to me? Did it make me feel better, and was it worth it? No. It hurts me to hear him say "See nothing I do is right."

I still love words and I love to play with them but now strive to use them with more kindness, love, and understanding. Knowing that people are all in different places on any given day and things that you say can impact a person more than you may realize.

Judgement is a strong, harsh word that those with any mental illness know all too well. Being judged is a big fear that comes with living with a mental illness; not only for the person who has the mental illness but also with the loved ones of that person. Mental Illness carries a stigma in this society that puts up barriers. It can do a lot of damage and in some instances can even prevent someone suffering from a mental illness from seeking the help they need. This also carries over to the family members of people suffering from mental illness. I struggled with this and still do if I am honest about it. Who do I talk to about my stress, my issues and struggles I face being the advocate and support for my loved one? Who do I trust not to judge me or my spouse? Who is my support? Don't get me wrong I have an amazing family and friend base in my life, and I feel truly blessed and grateful for them. That being said it has been a challenge for me to know how much I can share or vent with people that I know and love. I wanted the people closest to me to get to know William for the man he is and not the disease he is living with.

Unfortunately, there is a stigma that is still associated with mental illness and I do not want people to judge my husband based on his diagnosis. Slowly as I become more educated, I let more and more people into our world. It is important to choose my words carefully and keep my emotions in check when talking about our journey to my friends and family. I didn't want to burden anyone with anything that would make people feel stressed or uncomfortable. And honestly, I just did not want to be judged either. I brought people into our lives a little at a time while educating them so that they would understand Bipolar Disorder is a disease, and over time, as I felt more comfortable in my knowledge and understanding, it became easier to talk to those close to me and share the struggles that we have and I also share our joys and accomplishments.

Third lesson learned:

Build a stable support system. I have learned the importance of support groups like The National Alliance on Mental Illness, NAMI. It is critical to find support with which you are comfortable. There are different NAMI family support groups and have many different options depending on what county and state in which you live. Check your employer community as well. Many companies have employee groups and offer counseling through Employee Assistance Programs. All of these are tools that you can use to help you from feeling overwhelmed in your journey through Bipolar Disorder or any other mental illness with your spouse or family member.

I found a group within the NAMI family support groups that was for spouses or partners of someone with Bipolar Disorder and found a safe place to vent to other people who were on my same journey. I was able to get input on how to deal with different situations I faced from people who had gone or were going through the exact same things. It is comforting to have such a great support group of people on all levels from NAMI to family and friends.

2020 has been a challenging year for everyone on many levels. It is hard not to feel overwhelmed with all that is happening in the world, and easy to get caught up in the negativity that surrounds us at every turn. COVID 19 has made things even more difficult for those who are living with a diagnosis of mental illness. COVID has taken away much of our social interaction which leads to isolation and depression. It has made scheduling medical appointments more challenging which is detrimental to the mental health of everyone.

So, what do I do to get myself through this journey during an unusually stressful year filled with turmoil and negativity? I set realistic goals for myself dealing with issues related to William's bipolar disorder and the status of the world we are living in 2020. I try to identify and tackle one issue at a time. I keep my lines of communication open with my friends and family, AND I HAVE LEARNED TO ASK FOR HELP WHEN I NEED IT. I am learning to be more flexible, less controlling, and creative in looking for solutions to whatever we are facing. I keep educating myself and others on Bipolar Disorder, hoping that more people will start understanding and there will be less judgement. But most of all, I practice self-care. I have learned that this above all other things is crucial in keeping myself in check while making sure that I am there for William when he needs me the most.

During this time of quarantine, it is extremely important to take care of my own mental health so that I can be a steady support system for William. I make sure that I have an outlet for my frustration and that I keep in contact with my friends and family in the safest way I can. It is hard for many people, especially in our current status, to practice self-care. We live in a fast-paced world with high-tech jobs, and busy lives. News media, computers, cell phones, traffic, families and the list goes on and on. We run ourselves ragged trying to manage it all. I have learned to prioritize. What really needs to get done today? What realistically can I do, and what can wait? I break tasks down into reasonable projects so that I have time to rest. I limit my news media time. I don't know about others but for me this year has been full of endless negative news. It's not that I don't want to know what is going on in the world, but I limit the amount I listen to or read and choose my sources carefully. I don't need to listen to political commentary for 8 hours at a time.

I look for at least one thing in every day that makes me stop and smile. I know some people smirk at that, but it truly helps me. Anything from a joke on social media, hearing a favorite song on the radio, watching my cat watch the squirrels outside or even that it is a sunny day. It is good for just general mental health but especially important if you live a stressful life or are living with mental illness either yourself or a loved one. I keep up on a hobby that makes me happy and feel productive - for me that is crocheting winter hats and donating them to homeless shelters. It lets me be creative and I know it is helping people.

Be as social as you can through these stressful times. Touch base with friends, family and co-workers often especially if you are working from home. It is easy to become isolated and retreat into your head. Help people when you can. Volunteer, join a church or work group, learn and grow as a person, and help others while keeping social during any challenging time. Start a group where you meet new people in hearing other people's journey through a mental illness diagnosis either for themselves or a loved one gives you new perspective. Meeting with others lets you know that you are not alone, and this can be used as a resource when you hit a bump in the road and feel like you don't know where to turn. Keeping balance in your life is critical to keeping yourself healthy so you can continue to be the support that your loved one needs. Don't beat yourself up for your mistakes. Everyone makes them, no one is perfect. The key is to not dwell on errors but learn from them and move forward. Educate yourself and make a plan that will help you in the future. That sounds like a simple thing to do…don't beat yourself up - just 'keep swimming'.

William often talks about the mistakes he has made in his life. We all do that, but he is not able to forgive himself, learn from his mistakes, and move forward. Everyone has regrets to some degree, things that we might have done differently if we could go back in time, but I am learning that for William these mistakes still weigh heavily on him and he carries that burden always in his head and in his heart. At first I just couldn't understand how or why he kept reliving these moments — why couldn't he just learn and move forward? It is hard to watch someone you love carry these burdens all the time. I do feel helpless at times because I know

I can't carry them for him. What I can do is talk with him, support him, and make sure that he can get the therapy he needs to work through and hopefully resolve them.

All people face times of hardship and prosperity. There are times of turbulence and times of stability. I have learned that the path you take in life no matter its bumps is always better with someone you love and trust. No matter what challenges you face on any given day a person who cares for you will always have your back. I have that person in William. When one of us is having a bad day no words need to be spoken. We just sit beside each other and hold hands. We feel a peace between us that comforts and empowers us. It's that feeling that makes all the turmoil both in the whole world and in our little world stop for a moment. And we are just where we need to be at that moment in time.

As I have been writing I have been thinking a lot about my journey, our journey, and wondering if I would change any part of it in the hope that it would make things easier. I don't think I would. I think, honestly, if I would have asked myself that question at the beginning of writing this story, I might have found something to change. Now I realize this path we are traveling on, in this life, is where we are meant to be. Right here, right now. All of the challenges, setbacks, and disappointments have made us who we are. We grow in our love and our strength and we find that there is a beauty in our bipolar journey. No, I wouldn't change anything for the world. William has made me a better person.

My wish is that others will see our unity, our love, and know, if life takes them on a similar journey there is always hope.

Why Poetry is Arranged by Season

We have placed the poetry by season because a change in season changes the way a bipolar person feels and responds.

Spring

In my bipolar world spring is a time to come out of my shell. It is a time where I emerge from dark days and long nights. It is long past the memories of the Christmas holiday season. A time that can be daunting, challenging, exhilarating all in the same day.

Holidays sometimes remind me of never finishing college to become a psychologist. Sometimes it reminds me of all I am not, and all I wish I was. Things I have done or not done; those thoughts can be very strong in the winter. Spring gives birth to grass, and blooming trees, the ability to be outdoors more, to hike, to camp, to roll down the window and take in the crisp air. Morning dew, and friendly sunshine. Pleasant evenings, with the soft sunset. It sometimes gives birth to more poems that are lighter.

Summer

Summer in the bipolar world is a time when days are warm, we look forward to summer holidays, beaches, fishing, family gatherings, grilling out. Road trips. Outdoor events and celebrations. Summer rain and thunderstorms are soothing to the soul. Rains wash away the stress of the day.

And reminds me of times spent in the boundary waters canoe area with my family. The bustle of small tourist towns. The waves of Lake Superior and ships that sail on her. Times spent at John's Breezy Point in Larsmont, Minnesota on Lake Superior, and the smoked fish we shared in the cabin. Summer also reminds me of the song of seagulls as they fly in the afternoon sky.

Fall

Fall to me in my bipolar world is a time when people return to schools and colleges.

The fall leaves turn to dazzle our eyes and leave us with fond memories. There are hiking trails to be had and conquered. There is a time for fall camping, and campfires, the smell of smoke in the woods, Cascading waterfalls, and a majestic lighthouse on a cliff.

We move through a time of harvest to November when fierce storms show up on the great lakes to show their mighty hands of power. It is also the time when light fades away and nights become longer.

Fall is the most difficult season for me, sometimes it is a fearful time. Unconscious fears erupt without warning, a time when self-examination begins.

Winter

Winter is a dark time for me. All is cold and unfeeling; we move to the Christmas holiday and we draw close to family and friends to dull our pain. Anxiety rises. Our sense of failure begins to creep in and tries to communicate with us. Tries to convince us of things, that may or may not be true. Our words on paper become more critical. There are traditions in these months for many people.

As the Holiday season appears I think about those who have and those who are in need. I think about people that know God is real and those who have believed and doubt their faith. I try to remember days with family and friends and traditions we've held onto. I remember the dinners that often came and went so fast. And every year the ball dropping on new years eve. Exciting and disappointing at the same time.

Spring

3.19.2009 5:45 pm

The following is an Internal observation.

About Him

On the wings of eternal shore,
is his mind and heart waiting for her?
He is complex and simple,
never to be figured out completely, but only by her.
In His mind is her life, and she drives him.
The flowers shout out for him to stop,
and they wish for him.
For the one who will open his heart up completely,
in the rain that is failing.
He is softer than cotton and the clouds.
In the sky, thus all that we know.
And the man his focus is her, shining from all sea to sea.
Walking in the night his heart screams out her name.
And since her calling he has never been the same.
The family of old does not recognize him.
And the wind it rushes in to fill his heart,
but cannot get in, it knows it is dead for now.
For he is a machine without feeling, until that day when she arrives,
and holds out her hand,
and welcomes him home as hers.
She brings him to life.
Skies are calling him home,
how to reach him we do not know, and we wait.
For the sun is setting on life,
and we watch for the sign of the new.

The road beckons the call of the future,
and he waits.
His heart yearns with all the universe at hand.
Stars are calling to his home.
In him is the life of all of we know.
And his heart with the tears of the ocean,
goes deep and forever.
Where is the one who can hold that all in all?
And when will she be in his life forever, and take him as her life
and all?

My interpretation of a hope for love.

The Forest...

In the Forest is I, and the winds blows.
And the tale of the day, I walk alone again.
Rocks cry out and the tress are there.
She is not near, even though I see her there,
face and all.
The sun will shine again.
Will she walk to my heart?
Will she make her home in me?
The invisible does come, and the sun rests upon the sky.
She is not here now.
I wonder how, I wonder when,
that one will come alive in life.
Skies that snow, and the heart is a machine,
sleeping with the city.
For the longing that waves in prairie grasses,
tell of tomorrow.
The hope I have for that unconditional love for eternity.

Summer

9;5.2008   6:40 am

The following speaks of how a prospective love might be.

Beautiful...

Beautiful is the morning sunlight,
that cast its gentle light, on my maiden to be.
Fair is the day, to lend itself a hand, and hope to all.
Crisp is the air to which I draw in,
and in turn take in reminiscence.

Longing for just the smile of my fair maiden.
Walk on must I, to cast on the shadows I cannot see.
Will thine eyes ever feel the bliss,
that is cast forth from me?
Will thine heart, soft and tender,
stay so forever for me?
I shall earnestly, wait in green pastures, for your arrival.
No other place so deserving.
Shall you arrive by eve?
I shall prepare warm hospitality, to compensate your kind journey.
Beautiful is the morning sunlight,
that cast its gentle light on my maiden to be.
Will thine heart, soft and tender,
stay so forever for me?

9.18.2009 2:50 pm

My interpretation of my wish for forgiveness and remorse in life.

Wishing for Forgiveness

This desk no longer speaks for me.
Though it knows more than I do.
And I'm sure it's seen the faces of many.
Today I am the only one sitting here,
I don't want to die here.
I see out the window,
that tower behind which I left my future.
I have won this spin with guilt.
Many days for many years up until now,
I have collected cobwebs of guilt.
I have had much to offer, taken much,
and much has been taken from me.
Too young to have it taken from me,
too old to give it back.
Wishing repentance, and forgiveness for my soul.

9.21.2009   4:32 pm

A morning observation of family and home.

Sunday

Its early and kids sleep as the sun rises.
This week has kissed my feet many times.
The fall pageant of learning has begun.
Even though I fear I may know less than yesterday.
Bird chirp, kitchen is quiet.
The smell of coffee nuzzles my senses.
Ready now we head off to church.
All words float from the pulpit to me,
and I am reminded of my youth.
If only God would grant me time to make corrections.
Filing out, shaking hands, smiles, hugs.
A return to home, peeling of my suitcoat.
Dinner, family, football, a nap.
An evening playing board games.
Monday will arrive too soon.

Autumn/Fall

11.09.2009 5:24 pm

I am writing to the disease.

Stigma

I am here at the edge, of what was once here.

Water used to flow, and I set sail to the end of this day.

Drifting silence, heading north to a land I do not know.

Where will I be in that final hour,

passing lifeless flowers.

Where will the wind shake a tree, and lend a limb to me?

Intel says there is no one home,

and the path is still unknown.

Words carve into my skin, and I am alone again.

Piercing rain divides my soul,

as those looks of my mind debrief.

Time clock fades in and I am running, sunset pulls, this journey stirs me.

Some say he needs to be here, and others say not.

The Judas kiss left for me in a parking lot.

Other rain says it's all insane.

All in all, it's about what we gain.

Games of plenty star in several parades.

Colors multiply as I draw my shades.

I am here, why can't you see ME?

Where can we go to avoid this?

Stand still and continue to fight!

Winter

12.10.2009   2:55 pm

A view of a daily cycle of thoughts.

Crash

Afternoon has come, and she has gone.
Soul after soul.
Please come again, dont leave me,
these walls are too thin.
If after all I have done only adds to this?
If the afterthought should be so upsetting.
Can I, could I see the way home.
Again, and again the river flows back to me.
And I can't see past the shadows.
If I could cut through the air beyond my window.
Windows say, his heart is heavy with loss.
Crystalized pains.
Tears that reign.
Until sunset, I crash until I sleep.

1.4.2010   1:54 pm

A hope for a better future.

Confusion

We build new to reach the sky.
Not realizing we've become old.
Men's wisdom has become contempt.
As we call ourselves United,
We were buried by the two greats that fell.
One-man army in the middle of the street.
As they tricked us all in to believing.
Confusion, too many voices mixed by signals,
Silenced with fire.
Armed forces on the knee,
trying to believe we all have life.
In these moments is when unbelief speaks to us.
Rescued from the dark, and all that is measured.
This is where we meet, living in our dreams.

My Interpretation of dilemmas in life.

Adversity

Why is adversity the greatest healer?
Distance does not bring close enough,
what in mere tears I can't express,
in having a hardened heart.
I am reaching in to try to open the hardness,
not caused by you.
But in all I have expended to others,
and gained no return unto me.
Which I in turn feel selfish.
I have learned to carry greater knowledge with me.
As pain tries to open that door forward,
into the world of others again.
So, I am bound by fear of feeling pain, and joy,
swinging forth on a pendulum.
I have numbed myself to live,
and joked to pass time.
Will I love again?
Or has the dagger of life cut my heart in two?
Probably just my baggage, I have to throw, you know.
The honest seem to suffer most.
In the end of this day I am bound by integrity and loss.
Humility, I do not know if I am qualified for such a grace.

2.12.2010   2:20 pm

A visual distortion of emotional upheaval.

Faces of Life

Studying life from the easy chair.
And still we are all dreaming.
Drag races on the freeway.
Heading to the only home we've known.
I can't remember the last time
I was pegged/tackled for being sane.
Being level is not the issue.
Run me home.
Beat you there.
Melting minds.
I see my face in the window as a mirror.
Soft then flows the rain from the sky.
I have never seen so many faces.

Spring

4.5.2010   1:28 am

An observation of family memories.

Somehow

Look at all the smiles, and all the while somehow, we made it.
When the winds of time came in,
and we grew older, love came in to stand.
There are too many days,
we have drifted but we still remember when,
sitting on the same rocky shore,
but today, this time by an open door.
All wondering what life will bring next,
not wanting to leave any sense of home.
And in the midday,
we came to say we still are family somehow.
Putting the stress aside, welcoming the laughter in.
Sharing a helping hand in a story or two,
no matter if old or new.
And with each hour that passes by,
we somehow wonder why the life we have is so short.
Someday our time will come, and this day will be done.
Heading home that final time, to be together forever.

My Interpretation of celebration of life.

We Dance On ...

Oh, I felt something coming on.
Out the window went the day.
Around the world I could say.
Step and stomp I went my way.
I love the night that comes so close.
Lights that blink on and off,
like water from a hose.
And with every single step I take.
I feel like fall when we dance.
Down the sidewalk I go with my coat.
Hey, it's my day, let me gloat!
Friday is never something to see and fear.
The end of each week, it's so dear!
Heck if this thing makes any sense.
From which I came, gone and hence.
Whap a whoodle, is something new.
Sure, I know my daughter likes to doodle.
Saturday, I feel is coming on.
Its late Friday night and we dance on.

A poem just for fun, written on a good day.

Yardwork and Guys...

Morning came right up, and I got up.
Had some things to do, invited a neighbor or two.
To spiff my yard and make it clean.
I poured a cup of coffee and went outside.
Yea its early! A quarter to nine and grabbed that rake.
Started in the corner,
to make sure things wouldn't look the same.
And little did I know two hours later,
my neighbor called my name.
He grabbed a rake and hoe, I told him where to go.
To the Garden, and till all those old vines underground.
He huffed and puffed, but when he worked,
he didn't make a sound.
Little did I know, he brought his neighbor Joe,
And at high noon, they're already sucking on some suds.
My wife from the window said,
there are worse things to dread.
Why don't you go there, and have a brew for yourself?
Turning a little red, I believed what she said.
And placed my rake, in the garage near a shelf.
And once again, my wife came out smiling,
With half a steer on a plate.
Five neighbors and me, the wife,
went waddling through the back gate.
Had a keg of beer, hey how'd that get here,
a little bit of lovely steer.

Didn't feel quite the same the rest of the day.
But as we drank more beer,
our thoughts became more clear.
You should have seen our yard that day.
We cut half the trees down,
that's when the wife frowned,
and none of us could get away.
For little did I know, she was on the go, on the phone,
telling our wives about the mistake.
So, we drank more beer, rake there and here,
But ran into too many big ole logs.
Al grabbed an ax, and took several whacks,
and before we knew, it was suddenly all piled up.
Hot summer afternoon, made us all, look like goons,
Must have been the alcohol acting up.
And evening came,
and the yard looked pretty much the same.
Except for the Tree fort we build in the back yard!
We all stopped and stared,
"Who the heck went to Menards?" My wife exclaimed!
Not knowing what to do, we grabbed the keg or two,
and loaded everyone in the truck.
Took off down the street, wondering who we'd meet.
And then I thought I heard someone snore.
And the next thing up, someone poked me in the gut,
And said, "hey get up,

we got to pack our gear and head home!"
All I can say, that beer we had yesterday, did me in.
I walked in the door at a quarter to four,
before the sun greeted me for the day.
I asked Mary Lee, how'd the yard get clean?
She said all the wives stayed up all night,
And raked the yard with flashlights,
the whole night without pay.
Before I could lay down, she turned right around, and said,
  "Now it's your turn to start the housework for the Day!"

A desire for others to not make comparisons about me.

Can't Compare Me to Someone/Something...

Can't compare me to someone.
How can you measure me to someone?
Can't compare me to something?
How do you measure me to something that's not there?
Even nothing is something, when all is laid bare.
When looking at all backwards, in rewind
it always seems clear.
And when looking towards forward,
living in shadows of others causes the fear.
Tell me there is no reason, to face the future,
for the cause that is not me.
How do you keep reminding, and contemplating?
What and why can't I be?
It's there in all the pictures, telling your life,
and what is not mine.
Pride befalls all ignorance,
and leaves the life you lead totally blind.
So, I look out the window,
the rain keeps falling, into the night.
Somehow what little I have reminds me,
of what I shall, or what I might be,
or remember what I do have.
With each mornings light.

5.6.2010 12:15 am

My plea for love.

Without You...

Santa Clause once lived in the land of Oz.
And if you think I won't understand,
Just take the day and my hand.

If you think I wouldn't, I have already fallen in love with you.
Weeping behind the curtain.
Not much will make sense in this world without you.

Summer

9.2.2012   8:00 am

A writing as a result of a confusing end to a relationship.

Scratch

You got away with it.
It makes no sense.
You have lost, more than you knew.
You threw away the key.
I have learned, there's no way out.
Much more difficult for me, to see.
Love.
You got away.
And never came back.
I live the dream you're here.
It makes no sense.
If only I could connect.
It's all a mess.
Lines etched everywhere.
Come and go, as you will.
Because you are able.
Love with you, it isn't fair.

9.13.2010   7:20

A description of the illness.

Simply Bipolar...

Yes, I tell you there is an entrance to my mind.
It's difficult for me to see the ruts,
in the road, not always flat pavement.
Transformation of information,
is two times the speed of sound in slow motion.
What ride would you like to go on here?
Emotions shifting faster than a set of racecars at Talladega four wide.
And then there is that day.
Plateau. Calm. Numb. Empty.
But you fight because life is here.
Filter everything you are able.
You fight because people say what they do.
You dig your hoofs into the ground and pull forward,
into a new day, minute, hour, second.

Autumn/Fall

10.21.2010   10:24 pm

A mindset due to a loss in my life.

Cold

O dark side of my soul.
This very hour,
I am reminded of what I am not.
You rear your ugly head and tell me things.
You scatter seed in the sand.
And with the snap of a finger,
comes a whirlwind.
Everything I planted to hide behind is gone.
All I toiled with has been taken.
Be as so kind to let me be alive, and not alone.
I ask for forgiveness for my sins as they haunt.
Words I have dropped like molasses.
And pain I can't remove,
without your complete unjudging love.

10.16.2010   7:03 pm

Could be viewed as the chaos of life.

Broken

Don't lie, tell me why.
We all need love.
It causes pressure within you.
When to avoid the sins you must do.
And you ask why help, yes me, I am so free.
You're on the frontline, of design.
For falling farther than you know.
When we talk the day goes on and we walk,
past those who could love us the most.
And we end our evening with an empty toast.
So, to the next day we bring the weekend, we sing.
Sunday best, in loneliness.
Is it better to be here than somewhere else?
Where is it?
Will we be found?
As we push back all the tears,
and all the fears, time goes on.
I am found here a year later,
same emotions, same place.
Alone despite all the grace, connections disintegrated.
I am on the rebound,

asking more and more if I'll be found.
What can I do for my fellow man?
Shall I run and hide?
Shall I help?
Or come out from pain,
and bring them out from the pain?
Still, in this strange land I look at my empty hands.
And as sure as the starry sky, I see you go by.
And my heart is broken once more.
I've never understood the life I lived.
Old when young, young when old.
Always trying to be good.
Sit and be nice.
And then to make such a ruckus,
and those grave mistakes.
Two years of my life I want to forget.
I don't know why my children call me dad, or if they do.
I wonder if my family considers me family.
All I know at the end of the day, I feel alone.
All that's left is broken glass.

Chaos shows up in my life, this is another collection
of thoughts about it.

Chaos...

Fight the thoughts.
Split the mind in half.
Had too much of that cutting laugh.
Spent too many days being alone.
Had too much of being on my own.
Don't know if anyone is real.
Unsure if anyone really cares.
Sometimes all I feel is all the stares.
Wanting so much just to get away.
Wishing and hoping, believe me I pray.
Could it be our time has come?
Is this the end or when things have begun?
Is there anyone that can show us the way?
This time is blurry, sometimes we go,
sometimes we stay.

Some travel forward and some travel back.
People losing entire lives,
leaving homes while others pack.
Funds and jobs are getting low.
Tighter this rope becomes, hope it's not for show.
The more this happens, the farther we get.
Further from each other,
even though we walk close in step.
Why are the streets starting to fill?
Massive layoffs, spinoffs, and higher bills.
More collections, more churches full of praise.
In the end we are still the home of the free,
and the brave.

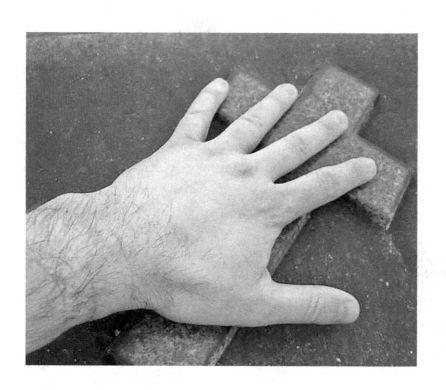

Winter

1.21.2010 (orig. 2.1.1995)   8:41 pm

Being aware of a place unknown that is uncomfortable.

Between Heaven and Earth

Again, and again I wander.
The more I uncover, understand,
the less I wish I knew.
Finding and believing,
you'd think it's quite revealing.
Sometimes knowledge is just a trap.
Going back and forth, right versus wrong.
Asking, what is it really?
Daily I grow in the knowledge,
of knowing less than I did yesterday.
Nobody can ever know the truth on this earth.
So, I hobble down the road, and listen to the toad.
And it sings of happiness and glee, in its own world.
If it knew how sad I was, would it cry with me?
Sometimes there is hell between heaven and earth.

A vision of a perceived relationship.

Visions of You, a Short Story...

Winter is coming, as I stand alone,
I close my eyes and dream of you.
Suddenly you appear out of nowhere,
and I run to where you are.
As I get closer, I realize the passion I have for you,
has drawn a shadow.
As I open my eyes the leaves rustle in the wind.
On the edge of the forest am I waiting for you now.
Turning and scanning the hills,
I wonder if you're on or behind one.
I hear your voice in the breath of wind, call my name.
My heart pounds and my body fills with gladness.
I can feel you now.
I wander through the trees to the river,
and kneel by babbling waters.
I look up and you are there,
my vision, my life on the edge of shore.
I walk to you, forever shines in your eyes,
to hold you I do forevermore.

12.6.2010 5:04 pm

Questioning someone's loyalty

Can I Fly

As I let you walk in my life.
There is a cloud to float on.
If I really knew the way.
I would not rely on yesterday.
And I have seen your face.
To light the way.
Will I have strength to carry on,
if you don't return?
Tell me what I don't understand.
Not asking you to hold my hand.
I thought I saw lightning in your eyes.
Sometime today I paused.
And I thought in your mind I got lost.
What is this? Is it a new song?
Can I fly, where I was yesterday?

An observation of a shared experience in a snowstorm.

Snowstorm

Let it snow more.
It sure is coming down outside.
Grab your coat and dress up.
For the sidewalk is ours to decide.
Which way to go.
Bring a camera, just in case we fall.
So, we can make an angel, or two.
Take my hand and let's run as fast as we can.
No need to fear the lightning in the sky.
Fluffy are the flakes that fall.
Soft and white, so real.
Don't stop at the corner.
We'll just keep running until,
we can't breathe any longer.
Fun in the snowstorm, is here.
The last thing the sky saw,
is a hug, from me to you.

Spring

5.11.2011   4:15

Change and the finality of love obtained.

Magic...

Stay for another day.
What is life really for?
In and out each door.
Pain and healing.
Dancing on the floor.
Does life seem fair?
Seasons on the change.
Our lives we try to make.
Daily rearrange.
Asking for heaven's sake.
Grab my hand, lets run.
Magic in the air.
Soon someone will come.
Saying I have loved you all along.

Summer

9-20-2011 5:15 pm

Understanding life is backwards, out of control and not always resolute. A hope for the better In life.

Backwards...

Come with me and we will see.
A road to backwards.
Where I have gone, I cannot go.
Looking back only makes me know.
Don't let me know, how
confusion and pain, walks right in.
Tell me how, I don't know, begin.
What do you see, in the light?
Harboring in the land of stage fright.
If I only knew what I should say.
Father to son, on this very day.
Can't let you go; the end is near.
Wish I could tell you, I am here.
Someday I knew this would all end.
Can't remember what I did when.
Looking deep in my soul.
Hope your life, in happiness, is an obtainable goal.
Come, go with me, so we can see.
Backwards the vision to set us all free.

Spring

5-9-2012   6:40pm

Feeling that there will be no resolution, even in remorse.

Awful...

They say a sinner's picture begins here.

Clawing and scratching, trying to make sense of things.

She left and took everything with her.

My heart longs for her.

All I know is I live under the same sky.

All I know is I wonder why.

Why would God let me live?

Eagles wings no longer comfort me.

The sun and the blue sky,

I hide from every day and hate.

Wishing there were more clouds.

Wishing she was back home with me.

Praying daily to God.

Obviously, I was not enough.

I could not do enough or be enough.

There is nothing for me now in this life.

Death knocks on the door with every tick of the clock.

Where have I gone, and where will I go?

Another soul abandons me.

And I am lost this time forever.

Winter

2.10.2012   1:50 am

A hope for change.

Change ...

Going to talk again.
Going to see again.
Going to walk again.
Going to be again.
Problem on the horizon.
What shall I do, where shall I go?
All the other days, I run and run.
Faster, faster and faster.
I keep ahead of the game.
No matter it keeps coming.
My hair is on fire, even in the wind.
All the other days I kept on running and running.
No matter what we do, we keep whistling.
We sing through the night.
All the other days, we did this again and again.
Made it to the other side of the road and back again.
Is this the way we change?

Summer

8.19.2012 8:40 am

A writing after an actual relationship ending, trying to stand my ground.

Goodbye

Woman I tell you don't be dancing round my town!
You're not welcome here.
Thought you could dance your way into my heart.
You're the one who tore us apart.
Funny how at the end of the day.
You thought you could come my way.
Really there's no reality with you.
There's nothing more you can do.
I should have stopped when I found out you were not free.
I should have just let you go.
Yet I knew you belonged to another.
You made that very clear.
Five years separated.
But it's the choice you could not make,
That made him yours, still near.

Not my problem and not my fault.

For all the guilt you got.

I should have run the other way.

I should have not let you have another day.

Why was I such a sucker for your pain?

There was nothing for me to gain.

All there was, was everything to lose.

Could not tell who's from who's.

After all was said and done,

you believe you were the one who won.

But little did you know; how much was lost.

Cause I'm the only one who knows the cost.

There's no sense of reality in your world.

You just carve your way by manipulation.

Goodbye forever, and good riddance.

Spring

3.5.2012 2:00 pm

Monotony in life that never ends.

Spring Never Comes....

Dirt and soot out the window, I can see.
Dirt and soot out the window.
Fog and clouds.
Empty trees.
And I think the rain will come.
What am I?
Spring never comes.
Jobs I've never gotten.
Happiness fleeting.
Things so willy-nilly.
Open the window maybe hear what's coming.
Open the window.
Nothing again.
Should I keep trying?

Again, and again, and again.
Snow still on the ground.
No wind to move my heart.
I'm merely a robot with twenty questions.
Hoping to make a go of this.
Will it ever take off?
Summer and winter came, threw me straight outside, fall I never saw.
Spring never comes for me.
And still I see out this window.
How is it others feel no pain?
Don't leave me, not abandoned,
not here not now, or ever please.
The weeks are too long between here and there.
Will spring ever come?

4.5.2013 1:46 pm

Stagnant

Open windows I can't see far, though I know what I've done.
Gone too far to explain now, or to run.
Open windows to catastrophes.
Hoping and praying now, life will have meaning.
And the rain it comes in now,
And leaves in a moment.
Can you stay a minute or two now?
Please don't leave me behind.
My heart and mind are toasted, on beveled plane.
Nothing will ever be the same.
I can't run and hide here,
Or go there forever.
What is right when all is behind me?
Neighbors chatter across the way,
Wish I was there.
Please don't run, run far away.
Past please come back to stay.
Unwind the doing that has been done.
So, I may feel safe.
Coming thunderstorms roam on the horizon,
And I see.
What I need is the peace of the lake.
Now stuck in a room with no grace.

Again, I look out the window

Winter

11.15.2013 10:45 pm

Gone

Walk away and then just tell me so.
Push all my buttons.
Dare you!
And you think you have control.
Little do you know I am better off unconscious.
Little do you know what death may bring to me.
Out of a living hell, hell I live now in.
Every day, every minute I die to live, live to die.
Death will never visit me too soon.
Hell is here forever.
Life is not something I can live.
Little do you know.
Little do I know.
Never will I live again.
Life will be gone soon.

11.15.2013 11:05 pm

My frustration and what people may say or view of me.

Shadows

Shadows no longer
hide me.
Nothing can save me.
There will never be a guide.
Rumors in the night lead me.
It's all gone.
Forever.
Work lies to keep me alive.
Miles before me.
Miles after.
On and on it goes.
Fields of harvest leave dust for miles.
Shadows walking in the clouds.
Nothing will save me.
Nothing will redeem me.
They call me a monster.
Scary, ugly, what's inside of me?
Free you see?
Complicated beyond belief.
What's inside of me?
This I always ask every day.

Spring

5.8.2014   8:00 pm

On edge

How many times have you heard me ask?
How many times have I tried to just keep breathing?
How many times have you heard me say?
How many times have I tried to let this go?
On the edge of no return.
How many times have I traveled this road alone?
How many people have passed me by?
How many times have you tried to tell me?
How many times have I fell?
I want to believe there something more.
On the edge of no return.
I can't go on.
How many times have you heard me cry out?
How many times have you heard my tears?
How many times have you seen my pain?
Trying to believe there's something more…
Trying to hear beyond this deafening sound.
On the edge of no return.
Fear grips my being, every single step I take.
How many times have you heard me cry out?
How many times have you heard me say?
How much have I worried for this person?
In a prison stuck for eternity.
All I can say and know is I need you now.

Winter
12.18.2010   2:55 pm

Get it from the horse

Ask him, like I know really.
This constant news of old.
Can't always teach an old dog new tricks.
Get it from the horse.
Can't lead it water, though how hard I tried.
Got a kick in the butt, and almost died.
From where I have come from, I don't know.
What is next and where will I go.
Why is it change drives us nuts?
Causes some to be strong, and others no guts.
All seems flaky no matter what we do.
I tell you I still want to be around you.
Long days ahead, nights too short.
Days I've felt before, years I've spent a float.
In the end it's still been said.
When there are more questions than answers.
Get it from the horse instead.

Autumn/Fall

11.15.2013 11:00 pm

Wondering if people have any realization of my existence and thoughts.

Speak

Be.
Do.
Speak.
There is nothing I know.
Nothing I'll ever be.
Nothing I'll ever do.
What is here is never there.
Let the sound rise, and my heart is destroyed forever.
If you only knew.
Let it be.
Just let it be please.
I never know.
I never knew.
Lost forever, beyond horizons.
Nowhere to escape.
A monster forever.
A heart lost in stone.
Gone forever.
If you only knew.
Let it be, they say.
It's totally torture.
It never ends.
My mind going over and over again.

I knew she was out there.
I loved her forever before I met her.
I love her now forever after.
If you only knew.
If only my heart could speak.

11.15.2013   11:22 pm

Time

Time is here and there.
Which way should I go?
Time.
Time to die, it's the only way.
Headed for the fall.
Time.
Three years of hell.
Time, yawn, smell, see.
What do you know?
It's my enemy. Time.
Time.
It's so short. They knew it all.
They asked all the questions.
They were nice when things were good for them.
Nice when the money was there.
Interested when I had a real job.
Tell me no lies, while I shift to the left or right,
depends upon you.
Time.
Shaking it all to the beat.

Let it light your night up.
Determine your path.
Time.

Autumn/Fall

11.15.2013   10:50 pm

A description of what it feels like to try and then fail in life.

On the Wrong Side of the Door

I am like a cat.

On the wrong side of the room.

Wrong side of a door.

Wrong side of life.

Wrong side of everything, with no chance.
No chance to recover.
No chance.
All is lost.
Lost at sea.
All of me.
Tell me what your spirit says.
You'll never change your mind.
I'll always be the monster.
A monster, scary monster.
Claws, and screeching.
Hair standing up on the back.
Tell me what you think I'd say.
No matter what you'd do.

Winter

12.13.2010   12:10 pm

Another Blue Day

I threw the lasso out last night.
To catch my life before it got away.
She looked at me and my mind and only laughed.
For in my heart there is much pain.
For it is still owned by her, even though she's gone.
My family does not know how to reach or repair me.
I have seen two families torn,
I am not ready for three, in my lifetime.
I mean well and tried hard.
But the pain the family and I bore,
has fanned the flame.
It burned the rope that ties us together.
She does not want her brethren.
She thinks she knows it all.
Her tempest lies in angst, materials and fame.
Only plastic walls, and charm are her character.
There is nothing solid about her.
I walk in the night and pray.
Pray for new family ties and mending.
And maybe, just maybe there may be a miracle.
A family made new this season.
To replace all that is lost.

11.16.2013 12:07 am

How life can just hit you by surprise and its impacts or changes.

Torn...

Got hit so hard I passed out
I want to run outside.
Can't now.
Seeing neighbors outside, I cry.
How could I let myself go from there to here?
Falling again and again.
How is it the will of others is stronger than me?
And they go on like nothing happened.
Life continues but not for me.
Wishing I was far, far away.
Everything turned up-side-down.
Roller coaster.
I have driven here many times.
Why not now?
Waiting forever has become tedious.
Tearing out many trails in my mind.
Pictures soon remind me.
Of what I've done and left behind.

9.23.2014   5:55 pm

A love lost.

If She Only Knew

I saw her, and after you asked,
"How could you do such a thing?"
Yes, love is so blind sometimes, but I did not care.
I saw her alone.
She was a vision.
She was my everything.
She said everything without one word.
She was in every dream of mine,
from childhood until I was a man.
She made me a man.
And that tale was only told for a moment in time by her.
So loud I had to cover my ears forever!
And there was love!
It was all I knew!
All I wanted to know.
My greatest fears came, when I lost her, in a whirlwind.
And my life disappeared.
Everything I knew,
Everything I thought,
Everything I hoped to become, gone.
And I dealt with it alone, as a man.
I have grown old in such a short time.
Not knowing if she still hurts, it kills me every day.
If only a rose could help her smile.
I would gladly give all for one teardrop that was shed.

Summary

9.20.2014   6:20 PM

A direction for the soul to remain humble and vigilant.

O Blessed Soul...

O blessed soul,
please remain so humble.
Stay on the path, even though so weary.
Magic happens in the woods,
and across the land.
People here and there hand in hand.
Shall I remember you my friends forever?
Shall I remember you forever?
May I know I'll never be alone.
For we are all here now.
Even in this quiet hour.
Rest may allude me.
But my strength, Oh God, you give in measure.
Many may fail me, many may judge.
There are some that stay.
Some that will play.
And some to be true.
Some will point that finger and cry," AH-HA!"
But I know in the end of the day we are all the same.
Wishing, hoping, wanting.
Will I be satisfied with just enough?

Autumn/Fall

10.16.2014 1:35 pm

Dealing with defeat in life.

An Onward Life...

Going into a no man's land.
I've been this way before, somewhat seeming lost.
I have tried many times to grow up.
And sometimes I have seemed to reach there.
And sometimes I seem to stay.
But there are many things that strike me down.
Time and time again.
Only reminding me of everything lost.
And I forget if I was ever loved.
I forget why I am alive.
I forget why I live.
Or why I even bother sometimes.
Saps all my strength.
Makes me mad, and I can do nothing about it.
Sometimes I cry in that church, so alone.
It's the only place, that church, where I feel I can come home.
It's the only place I feel loved.
It's the only place I am accepted as I am.
It's the only time I can live.

11.23.2014   3:35 pm

The motivations of people sometimes.

Judgement

Finally found the thing I was looking for.
The home that was lost the home that's here now, mine.
Here we go the end is near.
There is nothing to fear, here we go.
And off we run, to have some fun.
Here we go the end is near.
Here we go there is no fear.
Don't understand where I am in this lost land.
Trouble may come and where will I be?
Trouble will come, and they will see me.
Why do they judge the lost, and make me lose?
Why are they scared?
And what is it they must prove?

Winter

1.29.2015　3:50 pm

An asking for trust in love from another person.

Eye to Eye

Put your hand in my hand.
There's nothing you can't do.
Put your hand in my hand.
Let's take it and see it through.
Sitting on chairs eating a dinner made for two.
That's what this eve I'd like to do.
A walk down memory beach.
With you my sweet peach.
And when the sunset fades to grey.
All our cares will float away.
Into the night we go.
Staring eye to eye in the night.
Slowly you drift to sleep.
I can recall every breath you take.
And I'm able to find some peace.
Please give me your hand.
Never let it go, so that we will know,
forever is not just a word.

1.29.2015   3:09 pm

Friction in a relationship.

Unsure

Walking away from you.
Walking away from me.
Hello sunshine.
Feeling just so fine.
What you're gonna tell me?
Don't you tell me I'm far from home.
Though I've seen better days.
In many other ways, I'd rather be alone.
Hello sunshine. Me? Just fine.
What you gonna say?
Nothing is forever. That's the way life is.
Something's gotta give.
The way you think is right,
But for my mind its too tight.
Not the way I want to live.
In my world, when the clouds fade away,
it brings sunny skies.
Into the sunshine.
Hello to the moonlight.
Hello to every star in the sky.
Put your right hand up and swear your life away.
Cause what I want to give you is more than you can handle.
Why you ask?
Cause my life is here.

Spring

4.4.2015 2:50 pm

Struggles.

Empty

Gotta be able to shake this.
Off it goes out the window.
Flying towards the sky.
And it becomes a little cloudy.
I'm not really sure why.
Sometimes, I think God himself is testing me.
Sometimes I think I know why.
Often times I'm not sure if he loves me.
Often times I wonder why.
Am I alone in this struggle?
Can somebody, somewhere make sense of this life?

The lack of understanding from people, and the search for absolute answers In life.

Out of Control

Ding-dong, do you hear the bell ringing?

From the church on the hill.

Away I have strayed trying to find my way home.

How long have I been lost, forever?

And which way will I go from here?

The dawn of a new day does not solve my hearts tears.

And there are many miles between here and there.

They say I try to ignore it.

They say It'll pass.

But it's really been the same thing for years.

So it's a tissue I take from you.

To cover the miles of shame.

To cover reality and this never-ending game.

How can I find my way home?

No directions came with this life.

No instructions, or a book, or a manual.

How do I live?

Try to scrub it all away.

Try to explain it another day.

How much longer does this pain go on?

Autumn/Fall

11.23.2015   9:25 am

A hospital stay.

Journey...

All I knew is all I know.

That the world is never the same as it was.

It is flat, and there is a cliff.

And we can all fall off if not careful.

Or we can stand at the edge and wonder.

When the sun rises,

All I know is what I knew before.

Somehow, I must breathe.

I'm a survivor by habit.

The gift I had was lost long ago.

People say "Live!"

And I say I have.

They say, "You really don't live."

But they were not there in the rain.

They were not there in the snow, the fog, the hail and the wind.

They didn't sit with me by the shore.

I walked alone with God.

And all I knew is all I know.

That there was time to learn, to learn and grow.

A time so long to serve and give.

So long, I'd never had the chance to live.

It's no wonder when I became free.

And even that was taken from me.

I ended up behind brick walls.

And then the people came from nowhere.

And made my jagged world round.

So, I could walk all over the ground.

They didn't know me then.
They didn't want me, the way I became.
They wanted me behind that brick wall.

But I wanted to be out in the sun, on the beach,
and on the road.
I could outrun them all, and they didn't like that either.
There's no happy medium, but they still say,
"We want you to be strong and happy…"

I shall return, not to the place I was, but to the place I'm going.

Winter

1.30.2016   12:30 am

My thoughts, struggles, questioning, wrestling, will things get better?

Inside Me

You can't see the swirl.
You can't see the pain.
You can't see me scream inside.
You can't see inside my head.
You can't see the double vision.
You can't see my contradictions.
You can't see my love.
You can see my every worry.
You can see my concern.
You can see my mindful convulsions.
You can see me here.
Can you see them run?
Can you see the judgmental daylight?
Can you see their puns?
I have traveled through many valleys.
I have traveled mostly by night.
I have traveled through short time history.
I've been saved by His might.
Will I ever see the doorway?
Will I ever smile?
Will I get to rest in this hour?
Will you stay a while?
Will you tell me that you love me?
Will you stay right here?
Will you tell me this final hour?
Forever can be here beyond today.

1.30.2016   12:55 pm

A feeling that life is constantly out of control.

Stuck Here

I remember when I was young,
and I would run so far from here.
On and on I was so strong, now the day scares me away.
And nobody knows me like I do, like you think.
The dawn of the other day opened the trap door
to my heart and mind.
The dawn of the other day was horrible.
I was not the one who walked away.
I pulled the cord, and all went to hell.
I could stop nothing and then I knew the world was so small.
And I could not keep them away.
And I ran the other direction so hard I hit the wall, despite my efforts.
Topple all the towers and street lights too, they all fell.
And there was nothing I could do, the trees in the forest spoke.
At the dawn of the new day I fell on the forest floor.
I crumpled up into a ball and cried myself to sleep.
I thought I'd join the auto club only to be thrown away.
Here they come.
Waiting for the doorbell behind this large door.
Ding Dong.
Wanting to walk away but stuck here.
I'm against it whatever it is.
Ding Dong
Ding Dong

2.9.2016   9:45 am

A decision to go a different direction In life.

Restart

I threw it away today.
Going all the way back.
It came from nowhere.
And I said enough was enough.
On the fair way, on the way back.
Nothing I could say.
Nothing I could do.
To get myself changed for you.
Keep on dancing to let it go.
Jumpin' on the big airplane.
Before I go insane.
Let all fly out.
And I thought I knew my name.
Became so weak, became so strong and then I knew.
Keep on dancing to let it go.
Let it fly.
Getin' on the big A train.
Going on my own track now.

2.10.2016   9:10 am

A relationship ending in total surprise, devastation, desertion.

It's Over

Don't stop now.
Go away.
Don't stop here today.
I told her on the airplane.
I found out his name.
And she understood why I've been so clammy.
Hit the dirt running so hard we knew what's up.
And what I have in store.
I told her this and that.
There's nothing you can do.
She said it's not you it's me.
And funny I thought I agreed.
So calm is the hurricane inside for now.
And then storm let loose when we hit the ground.
I ran away, far away.
And it was over before I knew what the sunset did to my face.

2.15.2016 2:15 pm

The end of a real relationship where much was Invested and lost.

Let me live

Someone took my nose and smashed it on the wall.
Thinking they're all that.
And I let it eat me.
For I was there, being dragged down.
A sentence I could not escape.
And now they all stand there wondering why.
You're so selfish.
Where are you now?
You are only scared of yourself now.
You made me cry.
But you did not see me.
You did not see the years of tears I cried.
You forgot that I was there.
So many times, over and over.

Over hill, over whales in the oceans.

I swam until I drowned.

So many times, so many words.

Let my sound rise up.

Free me from you following me around.

I am not your prisoner; I am not your foe.

I was once your friend, someone you used to know.

They take my life still even though they're gone.

They know where I travel and threaten to take me down.

Free me from your following me around.

Free my mind let me off the ground.

I was there to deal with your brand of death.

Leave me be, so I may take a breath.

It may be later, but this is my time now, you had yours before.

2.26.2016 2:50 pm

Looking back on life events and wishing things were different.

Desolate

Once there was a day.

When the earth was warm.

And they knew all was well.

Then I was born.

And all came to change.

All the smiles were, becoming.

And all the days were new.

And the light drew near.

And in those days' I grew.

When all was new.

I came to be, quite tall, but still small.

And when I was two-years-old I saw.

Out the window there was quite a scene,

the world was old, and new it seemed.

And then I saw from the couch standing there,

out the windowpane, there was a train,

and I smiled back at them.

Tell me, where did we all go then?

Tell me, why does this day have to end?

Tell me why, all I once knew,

grows so cold, grows so old.

And I became a lost soul, never to return.

Tell me why then.

There are no grins, only tears,

filling the windows now.

2.21.2016 7:45 am

Simple frustration.

Listen

I told you once
Walk away.
I told you twice
I was trying to be nice.
I told you three times.
I was all yours, not mine.
I told you here
I told you there.
There's nothing wrong with your hair.
There's nothing wrong with you.
I told you.
I told you many times.
I was yours.
Why don't you listen to me?

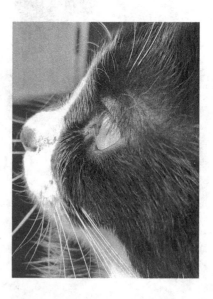

Thoughts of believing what people may have thought of me.

Crazy

Someone once said they could get inside my head.
But little did they know what was in there.
On the day I thought I knew.
On the day I thought was new.
A new day was dawning.
They said I was crazy, for thinking what I thought.
The things I should not ought.
The things I once had fought, and still am fighting.
The things once outside, the things I would often hide.
The things that I once knew inside my door.
The things I knew once more.

If only I knew what they were thinking.
I'd live a life worth living, according to them.
But little do they know I am a prisoner.
Under their control, I thought that I had escaped.
But little did I know, what I was in for.
I wish for a new day, and for certain things to go away.
O little did I know.
They thought I was crazy.
And so did I!

Spring

3.31.2016   10:20 am

A relationship that ended, but not in memory.

It's Never Over

Don't tell them what I must go through!
I'll never lose sight of you.
And that day I'll walk away.
And they'll end up with nothing to say
No matter what I seem to do.
All I know is I love you.
And that fateful day.
They'll say I walked away.
No matter what I try to do.
I'll always come right back to you.
I'll always be faster, stronger.
Running here, running there.
But yet I can't seem to get anywhere.

An interpretation of personal attack from another person, and dealing with their personal ego, or pride.

Frustration

Hey!

You told me to give it up.

Because you have more money than I do.

And you called me a fool.

No matter what I do.

There's nothing I can do to make it right!

Keep on dancing through the day and night.

Through the day and night keep it up.

No matter what I face, I must.

When the window is open you close it.

And the doors too.

Why is it your important in all you do?

You told me to give it up.

And then to give my all.

But it was never enough.

No matter what I do, there's nothing wrong with you.

Keep on dancing, to make it through the day.

I don't know of any other way.

Frustration is my cue to leave you.

But I don't, because I care,

even though you do what you do to me.

5.2.2016   9:15 am

My view of my daughter's life.

It Hurts

She's 17 now and in love.
Somehow, I feel second rate, second place,
and sometimes not at all.
Those pictures sit on the dresser,
and I wait for days to play with her.
Those pictures bring laughter to my life when we play.
But her love gave her a gift today.
And it hurts because I have been placed in second place.
All I thought about the world crumbles today.
And I am reminded about former years of failure.
All I can think of is what I am not, or what not I may be.

I played with my kids for many years.
And it's hard to see they have grown, and their interests changed.
I do not know how to reach them anymore.
It's like we're in rooms of glass where no words can be heard.
I long for the days we can play again.
But they are older, and I am lonly.
When will they come around?
All I know is this silence. It hurts.

5.5.2016   4:10 pm

Being in a state of constant disappointment wishing for better.

Today

Odd this thing, they call today.

Why did I not think about tomorrow yesterday?

For years I lived knowing tomorrow will be a new day.

And I lived for today, yesterday.

And I have not amounted to much.

I have strived to be much more.

But I have come up short, again and again.

What have I missed today?

What did I miss yesterday?

What will I miss tomorrow?

This path is not productive.

This path leads nowhere.

I was the same yesterday as today.

And my plans for tomorrow,

is to be better than I was yesterday

Better than last week.

Better than last month or last year.

Time has never been my friend.

It is a cruel ruler.

It takes and never gives back.

Even today.

Summer

8-23-2016 10:10 am

A real relationship in turmoil and doubt.

Nothing More

I once heard from a bird you would not walk away.
And there was a day you were not there.
So, I kept walking.
Tell me what you can say or do.
That would make me think of you.

All the toys in the world,
would never give me anything I need.
No money can buy the sky and then some.
Only your love would do.
So, tell me what you can say or do.
That would make me think of you.
All I have to say is you walked away.
They say that nothing is something.
And maybe that's all I have.

07-02-2017   2:24 pm

An observation of thoughts of my family growing up too fast and missing it.

The Past Catches Up with Me

Today I remember
Fifteen years ago.
Toy trains and bikes.
They remind me of when my kids loved me, and I knew it.
Now I am surrounded by silence and things they played with.
I try to reach out, texts, calls…
There now is silence, and I'm never sure why.
They say it's this generation.
They say it will pass.
Somehow, I don't buy it.
No words comfort the cracks in my soul.
No thoughts, no words, there's simply nothing.
And they live their lives.
I feel like a marble in a roulette wheel.
Being spun around waiting for my slot,
and my time to spend with them.
But somehow, I struggle to fit into the right slot at the right time.
And for moments I am close.
But they are busy with their lives.
I live from day to day as best as I know how.
My heart longs for my kids.
Somehow, I even fool my heart with busyness,
thinking I can get away with it.
But it eventually festers like a bacterial wound.
And I am lost.

7.15.2017   7:35 am

A real relationship ending and the feeling of abandonment.

Left Behind

Where did you go tonight?
How come I cannot fight the escape of your presence?
When did I come to know I was lost?
How did you know?
Why did you leave with nothing to guide me?
Cruel is this town.
Why did you leave all behind?
No future for me.
All you left is tears.
Can I recover from the day?
When there is nothing left to say.
Please come home.
When will I learn to live?
When will you learn to give?
Cascading under the waterfall of silence.
There is a new day.
But there is nothing left to say.
When will I grieve this loss?
I am left behind forever.

7.18.2017   7:50 am

The fear of being alone.

Fear...

When there is nobody around.
I have the greatest fear.
That my life will slip away, without someone to care for.
Or I'll be left alone to die.
When the door opens, I run away.
And there is nothing I can say.
And then the sun sets.
Outside it's so dark and cold.
Don't let me run away.
Don't let me escape.
Don't let me hide again.
Please let me call you more than friend.
And then there should be always more.
Don't let me out the door.
Even in your arms I am scared.
Don't let me run away.
Let me stay to see another day.
A long hug and a kiss will do.
All I want to hear is I love you.
Do what you can to make me stay.
Never let me run away.

Self-doubt.

Uneasy

I feel rushed in a panic.
Life is full of static.
My brain feels like a dusty attic.
When the rain starts falling.
Is there anyone I could start calling?
Where is there room to breathe?
Is this road gonna let me leave?
When the walls start to cave in.
Will I start misbehaving?
When the rocks all fall away?
When will be the end of my days?
When the wind calls my name.
Will I ever be the same?
When the moon starts rising.
Will I be compromising?
When the people start to tell me.
Will I still be loved by thee?
When the water rolls in from the sea.
Will you stay forever with me?

8.19.2017 8 am

What It feels like to be confused In life.

Confused

I'm not home today within my mind.
See my tears.
Can't say when enough is enough.
Alone on every plane.
Alone with the pain.
I not home today, never will be the same.
I'm not here, I'm not insane.
Can't find the words to describe how I feel.
Knowing I don't believe I am as old as I am.
My mind knows the difference.
In this world of shame and doubt.
Can't tell you what it's all about.
All I know it's not making sense.
Can you tell me when it will end?
Can you tell me you'll be my friend?
Cause if the night lasts too long.
I'll never sing a happy song.
When the sun shines through the day.
Will this feeling ever go away?
If I really knew what to do.
I think I could really walk with you.
I'm not home today, because it's too much to bear.
I'm not home today because there is nothing I could share.
If I really knew what to do.
I could tell you, what I could do.

Questioning where things are In life and when things might occur.

Questions

Where is now?

Where is there a place?

What is on my face?

Where does the day go?

What do I really know?

Is the sky about to fall?

What will I do through it all?

When does the pain stop?

Why does a rabbit hop?

Too many questions fill my day.

Someone please help me get this to go away.

Someone I hope will be my friend.

Someone to walk with to the end.

When the day is done?

Will I feel I have won?

What battle did I really face?

Hope I have not fallen from God's grace.

8.19.2017   8:55 am

The realization of self-worth versus what has been believed before, as told by another person of romantic interest or influence.

Stop

Who do you think you are?

Telling me what to do.

The worst thing about all.

Is you can't say I love you.

Many years have I stood on a distant shore.

Many times, you believed I could take more.

Manipulation is your main game.

In my head, simple.

In your head insane.

I can't run your race anymore.

So, this time when you ask, I'll close the door.

Thinking someday I'll give in.

By mere communication.

By a single word.

I'm beyond the end of my rope.

Have you not heard?

I'll stand here with my heels dug in.

And this time I'll be the one who grins.

Because I've learned from the past.

Your way will never last.

And so, in that case this is where I begin, and you end.

To live my life on my terms.

Not by your weapons.

Not on your every whim.

But my will this time. Not by your thoughts.

The discovery of love.

Know it, the Love is True

Turn around, before it gets you.

Know it before it tests you

Get it before it knows your plan.

See it before the sun rises.

And when it's here.

Know it's dear.

And then feel it.

Run to the finish line.

To know its time.

Don't spend a dime till you know it.

Get it before it runs over you.

Know it before the land gets wise.

Its ok to wear an emotional disguise,

but not for too long.

Know it's here, know it my dear.

My love is true.

It's never complicated.

Not conceded.

Know it's time we connected.

It's odd to explain when you have got, is all to gain.

What I told you is true.

My love for you.

Get it before it gets you.

Know it before it catches you.

Its ok to feel it now.

Its ok to tell how.

Know it.

Trying to walk away from things that hinder life.

Far from Bliss

I can't walk away from this anymore, even if I could.

I can't think about this anymore, even if I could.

I only want to run away.

I only want to end this day.

I can't do this anymore if I could.

I won't be that way anymore.

I won't see that way.

I won't be, well.

I can't walk away from this any more if I could.

I can't think about this anymore if I could.

If I run away I can make my day better.

If I drive away to the far away land,

I might be able to stand.

If I knew better.

If I was strong.

Then I'd probably know myself better all along.

Nothing here and nothing there.

It all leaves me with pain.

With nothing to gain.

I can't walk away from this anymore than I could.

I know I want to, and I wish I would.

If the day was near.

I think I could get over this fear.

I should just stop talking

I should just get walking.

I can do this…..It wont get me this time.

9.4.2017   8:40 am

Ttrying to understand life as it happens.

Whatever...

Want it!

I gotta get it!

Hear it!

I got to hear you speak.

Don't run away and save the day.

I'll still be here no matter what.

Can you?
Wish you knew the rest of the question.

Sunrise happens so fast.

Sunset never lasts.

Say it.

I'm gonna tell you any way.

It's not here.

I am telling you now.

No matter what.

Somehow this makes no sense.

We don't understand.

Frustrated now.

Autumn/Fall

12.2.2017   1:45 pm

Emotional sadness and remorse.

I Wish I Could Smile

I wish I could smile.
Far too many days have passed since I have seen the sun.
My sorrow drifts through the sky,
and I am covered in this darkness.
No matter how many times I say I am sorry,
No matter what I think.
No matter where I travel, am I free?
I wish I could smile.
Just like those who I have departed from.
But I am left with cold realities of being alone.
That one day when I could have said no,
this has brought me here.
That one day I let emotion be my logic.
That one day I was destroyed forever.
I still walk alone, no matter where I go, or whom I'm with.
No matter how much I say I'm sorry to the wind.
There are always storms now.
There is so much rain and cold.
No matter how much I want to say I'm sorry to her.
And I would....
No matter how sorry to any one person on this earth.
I wish I could smile.

Winter

1.28.2018   10:20 am

Unsure of the finalities of life.

If I Knew

Tell me what and I will do it.
Walking down the open road sometimes is an easy place to be.
Tell me where to be and I'll go.
Climbing the highest tree.
If I knew better, I would know and go.
Maybe do better things.
But there I go, and sometimes I am not there.
And I run, and I run to and from.
I wish I knew all that there was to know.
Sunrise, Sunset, Sunrise, Sunset.
It gets to be the same everyday
And if you knew all was well,
And if you knew every word I could tell.
Maybe there would be some peace.

Summer

7.29.2018   4:20 pm

Don't Know Why

Why don't you tell me?
Tell me to walk away.
There's nothing more for me to do
Suffering burnout.
You keep me here as a prisoner.
You think you keep me alive.
But I know better, my brain.
It's not sure it's me.
No matter what I do it says it's the big city.
Other self's say what to do.
Thunderstorms move me from here to there.
I'm a prisoner of the air.
There is no longer a star.
Only a prisoner from afar.
And this life I think I lead.
Is just too much for my little brain.
Too much to keep me sane.
No matter where I run.
I'll be burnt by the sun.
If only you knew, sad softer times.
On the lake, I live.
On sailboats, I dream.
Somehow there is peace.
Peace, from the prisoner, that Is me.

7.29.2018   3:25 pm

Past rejection from a religious community, before my current church.
This is not my belief of all religious communities.

I Knew Why You Did It

I knew why you did it.
Think it gave me more grace
I did not see it coming.
I left without a trace.
Your organization thinks its God.
Smashed the pumpkin, because you could smash no other.
Left all ashes on the ground.
I'm not here.
Never was.
Because I'm way ahead of you.
I protect myself.
You run away in fear.
You have no other choice.
You live no other place.
You never show any grace.
So, I run away.
Because I don't want to be your excuse.
You always choose the righteous side,
because you think your right and holy.
I knew why you did it.
Cause you care for nobody else.

8.28.2018 7:45 pm

The realization Bipolar Disorder will not take over my life.

A Requiem of Anger

You think you know me!
You are so far from lost!
I am no longer afraid of death.
Nor the tempest.
Nor the reaper.
I can go to the ends of the earth now.
There is no fear, for nothing can destroy me.
You sent me to the pit many times.
But God raised me.
You must acknowledge failure now.
My anger rides through the wind.
It propels me to my future.
You will no longer use it, it's mine now, I own it.
You are lower than the universe.

Autumn/Fall

9.23.2018   8:00 am

My thoughts of standing at the gates of heaven, asking for entrance, and acknowledgement of existence.

At the gate...

Oh, let me in I have no sin!

Oh, let me in I have no sin!

I have lived many days before!

I knew this kind of love.

Oh, let me in, Oh, let me in!

If this is the day I truly die.

Let me live without the lies!

Let me live with a little piece of youth.

This is not my miracle, it was yours all along!

All the angels have me tied up.

Please show me my mountain from inside.

A little piece of you lives in me, you made me.

Why would you let me go?

There was a time that the snow fell so deep.

And you were there.

Oh, let me in I have no sin!

Oh, let me in I have no sin!

I've lived many days before.

I knew this kind of love.

A little piece of you lives in me.

9-.0.2018   4:40 pm

My interpretation of a one-way conversation with bipolar disorder,
as if it was able to acknowledge its presence and effects.

Bipolar Mind.. Part One...

I'd wish you good morning,

but you can never make up your mind.

I can never tell what the day will hold with you.

I plan for good, but you seem to be the tempest.

It seems you have the first and last say.

My coffee calms me, but your already at work.

You remind me of what I am not, and what I can't do.

Even though my logic says I can.

You never allow me enough space.

You never allow me the time to be happy.

And just about the time I receive joy, you rip it away from me.

You tease me, I can never have a vacation from you.

Even on vacation you direct my steps and thoughts.

I try to remind myself of better places, but you point to death.

You interrupt my friendships, my family, my sleep.

If only I could go to the store and leave you in the parking lot.

You're just disturbing.

You say I am as well.

I know I could have been in better places, but you never let me go.

Not one hour passes and your still there.

Not one-minute passes, and you still speak.

They give me medications to outsmart you.

But you make your excuses, change your plans,

and leave doctors empty handed.

Go bother the devil, I'm sure he'd enjoy your company.

Another conversation with the illness of bipolar disorder,
telling it my raw emotional thoughts.

Bipolar Mind..Part Two...

Oh, you think you can just walk in!

Just like my best friends.

I think that you should really know.

You really, really, must go.

You have no right to be!

Or is it you cannot see?

A disease is one thing that I know!

You really, really, have to go.

You think you know me and make me live.

To the point I have nothing left to give.

Round and round each day I go.

And you, it's you think I should know.

If you'd just leave me alone, I think I might make it home.

You take my dreams and wash them all away

Until I have nothing left at all to say.

Bipolar mind what is it with you?

You stick to my life like glue.

You suck the life right out of me.

You take all I could be.

Go bother the devil and leave me alone.

Cause if I can help it, in me you'll never have a home.

10.7.2018 6:05 am

My Interpretation of what mental Illness may say to a person.

I Am Mental Illness...

I understand you, I know what you do,
I know where you live.
I do things that will mess with your mind.
I do things that make you unkind.
I do things and I know where you live.
I do things that cause you not to give.
I know who you are, you're not a star.
Do you think you can live?
I do things that get in your way.
I do things to ruin your day.
I do things to make you wish.
I do things that keep you in anguish.
Does your mind ever want to give up?
Does your mind ever want to blow up?
I know who you are, I know you are poor.
I want to make you give up.
I know who you are, I remind you of what you cannot be.
I remind you of how you'll always feel.
No matter what medications do.
I'll always be a part of you. Ha! Ha!
Doing things to lock you up, to block you up, to knock you up.
Doing things to place the blame, to make shame.
Doing things that make you never feel the same.
Repeat the same mistakes.
Repeat the same.
Repeat.

An understanding of depression.

Depression is a Bitch...

If your head hears it, ignore it, and hit the bed.
Depression is a bitch.
Walk it out and talk it out all, over town.
Drinking to cover it up, but it gets far worse this day.
Drinking makes my mind lose it, and makes it say:
Whatever you do, do it.
It doesn't matter where you go.
It doesn't matter what you say.
It does not matter if you live.
If your head hears it, ignore it, and hit the bed.
Phone rings off the hook instead.
I seem to ignore the world in this state.
Cause my mind rages in its own debate.
Its open town hall is full of air and noise.
Where nobody is there listening.
All alone.

An explanation of trying to live life despite life's appearances.

Tumble...

Gotta pick up the telephone, gonna tell them I'm not at home.

Gonna play hooky all day, with nothing to say.

Screaming coming from the factory, the day goes on.

Looking at all the smoke in the sky.

Creatures of the skies and land, they go on and on.

Master of the sky controls it all.

What will we ever do to live?

What will we ever say?

Going downtown to a lonely land, we can't really seem to stand.

Ship comes in to take all I own,

all I've seen, and ever known.

Why can't I balance it all in this home?

Where will I go to say it all?

What's going on, I don't really know.

What do they really say?

There's more life, there's a little hope around the corner.

See a little hope, see it there, maybe I'll really get there.

What will we really do, in the sand?

Falling from the sky uncontrollable we are.

My awareness of life's constant struggle, and realizations of that struggle.

The same game...

Here I go again, around the world without a friend.
And when there's nothing left to do.
I'll have a drink with you.
And when I get to where I cannot see.
I may think I just don't want to be alone.
And when I get to that point of grace.
I'll know I've ended up at the end of the race.
Around this world is one thing I know,
others seem to do and to know.
No matter what my hand tries to do,
There may be nothing to say, or nothing to do.
I cannot see my way around here, the place I once held so dear.
Confusion climbs upon my walls,
I run as fast as I can down many halls.
I think a doughnut and coffee might save the day.
But in the end, I still have nothing to say.
Some perks of life seem never to be around.
Silence is here, there is no sound.
So, I do it, live it, be it, want it when I'm home.
It's a disguise.
More than hours travel with me at work.
Even though I'm still out there, and I work on it.
I feel lost.

Will it end tomorrow?

I'll still be here.

Tomorrow will be here too with the tempest.

Off and on I try to touch it.

I work on it again, it never gives up, it's agitating.

Here, there, or at home its all the same game.

Always the same frustrating game.

A struggle after the death of my brother and its emotional turmoil.

Falling apart...

I don't want to feel this way, nor be this way.

My mind plays games all day long.

It's never happy, always reminds me I've failed.

No matter what they say, happiness is a challenge.

I've been many places, done many things.

But depression rules me, no matter what I do,

No matter where I go, or what I say.

Not even medications can save me sometimes.

I drink myself silly, only to make matters far worse.

Alcohol makes the world spin out of control.

Makes me spin out of control.

My grief for my brother now makes the world seem impossible.

Like I'll never climb that mountain again.

To be left for dead in the valley of nothing forever.

I have never been here before, I pray daily for a new normal.

I can't survive here much longer, or I will go backwards.

Back to a land I never wanted to be in, alone for sure.

I'm not sure why I feel cursed.

And I have nobody to blame.

Its excruciating.

Life is a task, a chore, every breath is challenging.

And at the same time, I feel like I am freefalling through the sky.

It makes me sick, dizzy, tired and so lost.

So desperate.

Winter

12.12.2018   8:24 pm

Personal thoughts and questions pertaining to life and the thoughts of others.

Chains...

I have stepped into the sun,
    and I lost my window.

And when the day is through, I ask?

When will I get out of this dream?

Is it so hard, to have lived?

Street cries, and she sings today.

What may come my way?

It's time to go town and see.

My question is what will everyone will say?

Clouds sure paint the sky different today.

There has never been so much noise.

Hitting so close, and so light.

Brave will we be in the end,

when we come to stay.

It doesn't make sense how to live sometimes.

Chains are binding my face again.

"Moms Story"

Do not worry I am strong in the noon day sun.

Sunflowers make nice companions.

I will always walk at your side.

The angels around me are treasures.

Sunrise is so pleasant; I will always be your friend.

Do not worry about where I have gone because I am not alone.

And where I sit is a peaceful place, all day long the love is strong.

I see many that I've known.

And they all have smiles.

But there will be a day when you will be called home.

And Ill be waiting here, to help bring you in.

Can you tell me why the distance makes you feel like I am not with you?

Have no fear, I am with you.

I miss you too.

I know how much you want to tell me things and talk.

Celebrate the life I have lived, I do.

Remember the memories, I will.

Live a good loving, humble life like I did.

And you will find peace, like I did.

Live and you will find life like I did.

Love your family, friends and neighbors and you will find love like I did.

Laugh like I did, and you will find joy.

I will always be with you. I am never as far as you think.

I am safe, loved and at peace.

Mom's Story was written by William for Marilyn's Memorial Service.

Marilyn and William in Two Harbors on Lake Superior, 7-21-2019

Mom was full of love, life and laughter.

She brought us to church every Sunday.

She was an excellent cook, like Grandma.

Mom had 8 grandchildren, and 2 great grandchildren.

She enjoyed every available time to spend with family.

She did not judge any family member or person she came across.

Family brought her joy.

Mom was a hugger. She would always say, I'm a hugger when
meeting new people.

She would listen to you, no matter the problem
and offer good advice.

And if she was unsure what to say, she said she would think about it
and get back to you.

She'd never blew you off. She loved everyone.

Mom enjoyed reading books.

She participated in the Zion Lutheran Church choir in Anoka, MN, and gained many friends there. She was proud of her participation in the choir.

She enjoyed small hole in the wall bars that served good beer, and Saturday night specials, whether it be pizza, prime rib, or burgers.

She enjoyed time away from the Twin Cities at their lake home in Two Harbors, Minnesota, on Lake Superior. Our family often gathered there for enjoyable weekend get togethers, full of joy, good food, and shenanigans.

Her death was sudden. She did not suffer. This sent the family into chaos because the anchor of our family was gone, and other members of the family were thrust into new roles, still leaves us with questions.

Mom was preceded in death by my brother Kris.

We'd like to think of Mom and Kris together in heaven.

Advice

Inside your head its a dangerous game
if you ever get out you're never the same
as when you went in
it's a shame it's a sin -
the faults that you have you'll never begin to understand
the battles you face and the demons
that hide in your own secret place.

So take my advise I know a few things-
don't trip yourself up life brings what it brings.
I am not saying you can't change your course
just don't make hasty decisions that bring you remorse.
Enjoy your journey from winter to spring-
Don't trip yourself up - life brings what it brings.

Liza Gunther Mueller
12/27/2003

Cover Artist

Jenny Evens has been a self-employed memorial artist in central Minnesota since 1987. Most of her work consists of creating finely detailed pen and ink drawings for customized personal monuments and Veteran's Memorials. She also does freelance portraits and portrait collages in black pencil, colorful mural painting in children's rooms and churches/schools, designs nature inspired essential oil diffusing jewelry, and creates original stained glass mosaics. But, she will probably be remembered most for her annual Christmas card art (which she considers her gift to herself) and has a large following of receivers who collect them.

In the near future Jenny plans to publish her Grandfather's Memoirs. He was a Swedish Immigrant who kept a diary of the adventures throughout his life (written in short story form) from his childhood in Sweden, through his coming to America in 1902, and the many historical, family life and social events experienced until his death in 1960.

Eventually, Jenny hopes to retire with her husband in northern Minnesota where she can spend more time hiking and enjoying nature with her camera, fishing with her husband, and have the time in her studio to delve into the ideas that are swimming around in her head just waiting to come out. She is currently looking into setting up a website business for her creative endeavors, but until that is completed, she can be reached by email at:

JEvensArtist@gmail.com

CPSIA information can be obtained
at www.ICGtesting.com
Printed in the USA
JSHW081203211122
33513JS00002B/61

9 781937 162184